LINCOLNSHIR
VILLAGE SIGN

BOOK ONE

Photographs: Fred Ham
Text: Shirley Addy and Maureen Long

Cover Design
AL PUBLICATIONS
Graphics Adviser: Mick Long

First Published 2003 by
A L Publications,
52 London Road, Kessingland,
Lowestoft, Suffolk, NR33 7PW
TEL: 01502 740 539

I.S.B.N. 0 9542950 1 3

Cover and Colour Centre Spread Printed by Rondor Print,
Lorne Park Rd., Lowestoft, Suffolk NR33 0RD
Tel 01502 564860

Typesetting and Inside Pages: AL Publications

INTRODUCTION

A L Publications are proud to publish this book of Lincolnshire signs with photographs by the late Fred Ham. Fred was a much-loved and respected member of the Village Sign Society, one of the Founder Members. He left his vast collection of photographs, slides, models, books, tapes and newspaper cuttings to the Society on his death in 2001. We are also grateful to his family, especially his two daughters, Trudy and Megan, for their help in packing and transporting the Collection.

When he died, Fred was working with us on books of Norfolk Signs, to finish the work started by Philippa Millar and the late Frances Proctor. Because he lived in King's Lynn, with one foot as it were in Lincolnshire, we have decided to do that county first, hoping to get the signs of his beloved North Norfolk into a more special production later.

Fred was always ready to share his vast expertise and knowledge of village signs with the Society members, as well as passing on spare photographs and slides and writing long letters to those interested in his hobby. He was always pleased to receive members' letters too, and would have been thrilled to know that now his Lincolnshire collection is to be shared with a wider circle of readers.

Fred was well-known all over East Anglia for his talks to numerous groups on Village Signs, history and folklore, as well as sharing his collection of unusual or humorous signs. He designed and raised the finance for the Islington village sign in Norfolk, when he was headmaster at Islington School. After his retirement, these talks and pursuing his photography for his hobby were his main occupations. He spent hours cataloguing and listing his collection, making it so much easier for us to find a particular slide or photograph quickly.

He was thrilled to see the birth of the Village Sign Society and was a Speaker , showing slides, at each of the Society's annual meetings he attended up to his death.

We miss him a great deal. On finding a new sign the first thought still is, "Must tell Fred about that!"

Thank you, Reader, for buying this book. Thank you, Fred, for making it possible.

Shirley Addy and Maureen Long, June 2003.

ALVINGHAM

Alvingham lies in rich agricultural land four miles north-east of Louth, in the Middle Marsh area. It was listed in the Domesday Book and its name means 'farmstead of a man called Aelf'. Gilbert of Sempringham, son of a Norman baron, founded his priory here in 1130, next to the site of the earlier Saxon church of 550AD. Details can be found in the Bodleian Library in the Alvingham Missal. The priory was busy and well-used until the plaque claimed most of its inhabitants, helping fill the Black death pit at nearby North Cockerington.

Local fields contain many of the old Priory stones. The Church of St. Adelwold shares the same churchyard with St. Mary's of N. Cockerington, since Hugo of Wells, Bishop of Lincoln in 1215, declared it to be a 'perpetual vicarage', served by one Vicar. St. Mary's is now under the care of the Historic Churches Trust, but St. Atholwold's still serves the spiritual needs of both villages, since it's restoration in 1933. Before that, it lay derelict for almost a century. There is a uniquely beautiful approach to the churches, over a bridge by one of the few remaining working water-mills and through a farmyard, so stout footwear is part of the worshippers' needs for much of the year. Through the churchyard lies the River Lud. a tranquil home for Louth Navigational canal, which carried ships past Lock Farm to the basin in Louth.

The mill, mentioned in the Domesday Book, helped provide the 'staff of life' to villagers for many centuries, and happily, it has now been beautifully restored and is open to the public and working at specified times There is a resident mill blacksmith, whose skills now are harnessed to more modern metalwork, close by the Old Forge.

The ancient village stocks were replaced by replicas in the Queen's Silver Jubilee Year on the site of the originals. A thriving Pottery and gift shop is a top tourist attraction, where the goods can be seen being made and hand-decorated.

There is an active Victorian Methodist Church, local shops and amenities, all the Time retaining a rural charm.

The sign, in metal, with the name in gold lettering, show village motifs in black, these being the two churches, the anvil and stocks, and a wheel depicting the water-mill.

BOURNE

Bourne means place at a spring or stream and was listed in the Domesday Book. It is a market town and the birthplace of Robert Mannyng in 1264. He was the first scholar to give shape and form to the English language as we know it today. Bourne church belonged to the Abbey where he lived and worked. Better known as Robert de Brunne (Robert of Bourne), because of his long association teaching at the Abbey. He died around the time that Chaucer was born, but to him we owe the understanding of Chaucer's work. Robert wrote in what he termed as 'simple speech for love of simple men'. According to Charles Kingsley, Hereward the Wake was reputedly born here too. It was in the twelfth century that the Augustinian Abbey was founded at Bourne. The nave of the Church has the only Norman remains built into it.

One of Lincolnshire's best sports grounds is in Bourne and it has been endowed by an ancient Charity at Abbey lawn. since 1770.

Another Charity has provided bread for the poor, after a schoolboys' race at White Bread Meadow. As the race proceeds, bids for the field are made and continue until the race finishes. The highest bidder holds the land for a year and gives his rent to the Charity.

One of the greatest feats of Roman engineering was carried out here, the Carr Dyke. This caught the drainage from the hills for 56 miles, holding it back from the Low Fens and discharging it into the River Nene at Peterborough and the River Witham near Lincoln. It can be seen at Bourne.

This place has lots of rich history, with the Roman Station, a Saxon stronghold, a Norman Abbey and moated castle, a massive keep with square towers.

The Norman Lords were the Wakes, descended from Hereward. Joan de Wake married Edward, the Black Prince, and so became the mother of Richard II.

Red Hall was the home of Sir John Thimberly, noted Roman Catholic leader. The Bull Inn, formerly a private residence, was the home of William Cecil, Lord Burghley, that great statesman of Queen Elizabeth I.

The village sign depicts the Town's crest, with lettering to show that the town is twinned with Doudeville in Normandy, flanked by the French and English flags.

BRANSTON

Branston is four miles from Lincoln on the B1188 to Sleaford. The name means 'farmstead of a man called Brandr' and was spelt in 1086 as *Branztuna*.

The Saxon tower of All Saints Church points to the long history of the now large village. Interesting pew ends include a pig playing the famous Lincolnshire bagpipes. Others show fighting monkeys and a fox with two dancers. The fourteenth century arch from tower to nave was opened out in

1876 when Sir Gilbert Scott restored the church and added a north aisle. The clerestory is 15th. century and the nave has a Tudor oak roof. North and South doorways and the font are 13th. century work.

The double-sided village sign was erected by the W.I. to commemorate their 70th Anniversary in 1987 and portrays the church and much of the past rich history of the village.

There are three former Rectories, one of which has an unusual garden feature in the form of a cock-fighting pit!

Villagers found it hard to forget the Rector's name, for the Curtois family provided 6 family members to fill the post for a period of 211 continuous years, surely a record. One built a schoolroom onto the church, another built a Georgian rectory in 1765. Atwill Curtois, a 19th. century Rector, was a skilled wood carver. He did the chancel screen, helped by one of his equally gifted daughters. She decorated the panels with snowdrops,

thistles, shamrock and roses. She also did a pageant of carved saints, representing 200 years of Christianity. The figures include Bishop Grosseteste, one of the builders of Lincoln Cathedral, which can be seen from the village.

The church gave the village too warm a welcome on Christmas Day 1962, when a fire broke out and caused severe damage. The church is now a lovely combination of 'Ancient and Modern'. There are two Halls. The old Hall, built in 1735 burned down in 1903 whilst the villagers were enjoying the Annual Goose Supper at the 'new' Hall. The old Hall was rebuilt as a private residence, whilst the later Hall is now a retirement home.

The lovely stream running through the village used to provide power for the waterwheel, still to be seen, which pumped water to the bigger houses.

CAISTOR

Caistor was listed in the Domesday Book, but existed much earlier as a walled Roman camp which succeeded a British hill fort. Ermine Street passed near it. Fragments of the Roman wall can be seen in the garden of the Grammar School's headmaster. Caistor (which means Roman camp) was mentioned by the Venerable Bede as an important Anglo-Saxon place and some mounds outside the town are reputed to be the site of the battle in AD 828, when the Mercians were defeated. The Church of Saints Peter and Paul has Anglo-Saxon and Norman elements, and there is a Roman well nearby. There are famous fresh water springs, the best being the Syfer Spring in Fountain Street.

Caistor is situated off the A46 between Great Grimsby and Market Rasen.

A "gad whip" is kept in the church and is one of only four still in existence. This whip formed an annual ceremony that was held until 1847. On Palm Sunday, a villager of Broughton fetched a large whip called a gad whip. This was made of wood, tapering towards the top. At the first lesson started, he cracked his whip three times at the door in the north porch. He then wrapped the throng round the stock of the whip and bound the whole whip with whip cord, using twigs of mountain ash. To the top of the whip stock was tied a small leather purse containing 24 silver pennies, later two shillings, now ten pence, and, placing the whole whip on his shoulder, he walked into the Hundon choir where he stood before the reading desk until the second lesson started. Then he waved the purse over the clergyman's head, knelt upon a cushion and continued in that position with the purse suspended over the clergyman's head until the lesson ended, when he returned to the choir. After the service ended, he carried the whip with purse to Hundon's manor house, where they remained. Caistor is a small market town surrounded by farming country.

Men from this small market town took part in the Lincolnshire Rising of 1536 and in the church is an effigy of Sir Edward Maddison, who was a leading figure in the fray.

The Fleece Inn is well-known for past Palm Sunday Fairs, when thousands of sheep were sold. Today it is ducklings dispatched in their thousands from the *Cherry Valley* production plant.

Caistor's village sign depicts the river surmounted by a tower of the Roman fort, with a gad whip and crook behind it, representing the fine church. The waves also form a hill and the wheat-sheaves symbolise the rich agricultural countryside surrounding the town. It tells us that Caistor is twinned with Sevione Leveque.

4

CHERRY WILLINGHAM

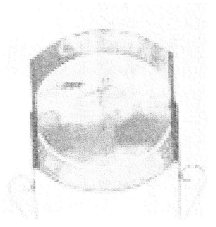

There are several Willinghams in the district. This village was given the first part of its name because there was once an orchard just below the church called Cherry Holt. Willingham means'homestead of a family or followers of a man called Willa'

The village has a long history, since Iron Age remains have been unearthed, along with medieval fishponds and a Roman Villa.

The church of St. Peter and St. Paul, depicted on the village sign, dates from 1753 , is made from Ancaster Limestone and stands on a mound. The spring line is below this mould, leading to some flooding, but the water was said to be a cure for weak eyes. There was formerly a ladle by the spring, attached to flagstones, then a pump was erected over the spring, but these have now disappeared.

Lincoln Red cattle are raised here and a barn in the centre of the village hosts a Harvest Festival service each year.

The peat bog is shown on the sign, along with the railway, which came in 1849, although there was never a station here and passengers had to walk or cycle to Reepham or take the ferry to Washingbrook .

There are now 2 public houses in the village, but it had none until the 1950s and '60s.

Cherry Willingham is twinned with the French village of La Grande Luce, near Mans. Every year either a coach load of English or French residents go to stay with their host families, forging friendships and lasting ties between the two.

The village erected its second sign, featured here, to celebrate the Jubilee of Queen Elizabeth II. It has the same picture of the church, replicating and enhancing the first sign, which, in our picture is old and difficult to see. Since Fred Ham sadly died before then, the picture has been taken by Village Sign Society member Rex Chaston.

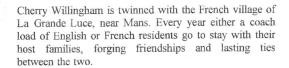

5

COWBIT

The village sign, which is a three-dimensional wooden carving, depicts the village name, Cu-bit, meaning 'cow enclosure,' with a cow, plus an anvil, denoting village crafts and industry.

Cowbit, pronounced 'Cubbit' by the locals, is a few miles from Spalding, east of Deeping Fen, looking over Cowbit Wash, often flooded by the Welland for months in winter and a popular haunt for skaters in frosty weather.

The church was built in 1487 by John Russell, Bishop of Lincoln. The sturdy tower is embellished by quatrefoils and there is a turret to its parapet. Rough stone walls of the chancel show its age, with equally ancient font and piscina. A large fish, carved in stone over one of the doors of the brick nave historically portrays the ancient Christian sign. Parish registers date back to 1561. There was also a Wesleyan Chapel in the village.

On the way to Crowland, in a garden at Brotherhouse, there is one of the stones which marked the boundary of the famous Crowland Abbey. St Guthlac's stone bears a Latin inscription.

6

CROWLAND

'Crulande' was a small island in the Fens. The name means 'tract of land at the river's edge'. .St Guthlac, a hermit with a talent to heal and counsel, from Repton in Derbyshire arrived at Anchor Church Field in a boat in about 699 AD. Crowland Abbey was built in 716 AD by Guthlac's relative, King Ethelbald of Mercia on this boggy settlement. The abbey was partly destroyed and has been rebuilt several times, and was once the wealthiest mitred abbey in Lincolnshire. A hundred and fifty years after it was established, it was burnt by the Danes, who murdered its Abbot at the altar. The Abbey has a fine bell, also named Guthlac, given by Thurcetel. Abbot Elgeric is said to have added another six bells, making the first peal in England, after his death in 975. The north part is now used as the Parish Church of St Mary with Saints Guthlac and Bartholomew. The abbey is shown on the village signs, one at each end of the village, along with the Trinity Bridge. This bridge has three semi-circles meeting at an apex and was built in the 14th century to replace the wooden triangular bridge. The bridge has a carved figure of Christ, which is reputed to have come from the abbey. The sign also welcomes visitors to the parish. Before the draining of the Fens the streets were waterways and it was at Crowland that the River Welland split into two streams. Richard Cough, the antiquarian, declared that the Trinity Bridge was "the greatest curiosity in Britain, if not in Europe".

The village sign also depicts the Guthlac Roll, a vellum roll depicting the life of St Guthlac in seventeen drawings, now in the British Museum.

It is thought that Hereward the Wake was buried here. There is a tablet, in the massive Norman church built by Joffrid and his successors in the shape of a cross, to William Hill, the Sexton, who lost his sight in a snowstorm going to fetch a substitute to take a service as the rector was ill. However, he carried on his duties for 17 years, although blind, till his death at 65. The original church was damaged by an earthquake in 1118 and partially burned down in 1143.

William the Conqueror gave an estate at Sawtry to Earl Waltheof, but later the Earl fell from grace and was executed in 1075. This execution differed from any other because the earl's head is said to have kept praying loudly after it had parted company with the rest of his body. William gave permission for the body to be buried in Crowland Abbey, and it was not long before pilgrims started to visit the tomb. This started an ecclesiastical controversy which led 12 years later to the coffin being opened, revealing inside the completely unblemished body of the earl with its head miraculously reunited with the body!

DEEPING ST. JAMES

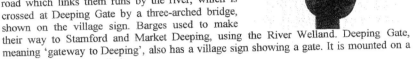

The name comes from Est Depinge and the Priory church of St. James and St. Benedict, founded in 1139 by Baldwin FitzGilbert, the Norman lord of the manor. In 1220 a charter was granted for a market to be held, on high ground to the west of the village, hence the two villages of Market Deeping and Deeping St. James came into being. The busy road which links them runs by the river, which is crossed at Deeping Gate by a three-arched bridge, shown on the village sign. Barges used to make their way to Stamford and Market Deeping, using the River Welland. Deeping Gate, meaning 'gateway to Deeping', also has a village sign showing a gate. It is mounted on a rounded cobblestone plinth.

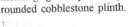

Just before the locks in Bridge Street, a house with a canal window was used to look out for the ships on the river. There is a village green and a lock-up, known today as The Cross, being the 15th. Century Market Cross, once used as a small meeting house and then used to house those of the villagers who were 'under the influence'.

The river was also used by a group formed by the District Nurse Langham, who in the thirties believed in a daily dip. Locally they were known as the Bathing Belles and gathered an audience. There have been Bronze Age and Roman finds here. The British Museum houses a Bronze Age cinerary urn, whilst Roman links include the Carr Dyke Crossing with the river.

Wildfowlers are attracted to the Mere, near the station, where willow has always been prolific.

The village is mainly an agricultural area, with an Annual Show, as well as a Carnival. By the bridge in Bridge Street is the ancient Cave Abhullam Baptist church, founded by a former Vicar The Rev. E.Tryon, who founded an independent place of worship after disagreeing with traditional church doctrines.

The Church of St. James, gives the village its name plus the Deeping, meaning 'deep or low place'. The building is Norman and medieval with an 18th Century tower and high spire. There is an unusual tub-shaped Norman font as well as figures to commemorate Baldwin de Wak, founder of the Priory and Richard de Rulos, Norman Lord of the Manor, who first thought of draining the marshy fens to create the rich agricultural and horticultural area of today. The church, also featured on the sign, houses an unusual shelter, like a sentry box, used by a former vicar to conduct funerals in the rain!

FENTON

This village is listed in the Domesday Book, its name meaning 'farmstead in a fen'. It lies between two tributaries of the River Witham and has a rich history, happily recorded for us on the village sign, erected in 2001.

The sign has a coloured shield-shaped design on a white background and shows four quarters, with a circular inset at the centre, depicting All Saints Church, which was restored in 1875. At the top there is another centre small shield showing the arms of the Lucas family.

The top left quarter depicts a Roman Soldier to commemorate the Roman occupation, whilst the right reminds us that the Vikings too were here.

The bottom left panel has a Crusader knight in front of an ancient arch.

The fourth quarter depicts the agricultural aspect of the village, with a Lincoln Red Cow in the foreground, with a back-cloth of cornfield , tulips, Church and Mill.

The nameplate and date are below in bold black lettering on the white background. There is also a small, protective white canopy at the top, altogether a most attractive sign.

HAXEY

In the Domesday Book of 1086 the village name was spelt as Achesela, in 1285 as Axaia and in 1373 as Hakesay, and it was formerly the capital of the Isle of Axholme. The name means 'mooring site at the river' or 'Isle on dry ground on marsh of a man called Hakr'.

Today Haxey is the largest village in the Isle of Axholme and has been established before the Conquest. Since medieval times it has produced flax and its production rose with the success of the textile industry. In 1740 a fire destroyed much of the village.

The Church of St. Nicholas was restored in the 15th. century. It has a 500 -year-old tower a hundred foot high, with a peal of seven bells. A recessed tomb in the chapel has a stone figure of a priest on it and above, on the wall, is an ancient Charter of 1336, granting a gift of land from Maud, wife of Walter de Brunham of Haxey. One incumbent here, Spenser Madan, was a chaplain to George III first and after leaving the village, he became Bishop of Bristol.

There are ancient stones around the village, relics of historical Fairs and Markets. One, on the Green, is carved with the arms of Mowbray, the exiled Duke of Norfolk.

Two customs have been observed in the village from medieval times. One is the ancient agricultural method of strip farming, when crops are sown in parallel strips sixteen and a half feet wide, half an acre in area. This still happens in some Suffolk villages also.

The other custom is the famous annual 'Haxey Hood' game, when a sport something like Rugby was played with the neighbouring village of Westwoodside, but a hood was used instead of a ball. This continues to happen every year on January 6th, the Feast of Epiphany. The winning side in this rough and tumble game carry the hood to their favourite public house to celebrate.

The village sign, marked 'Haxey Parish' depicts much of this rich history. The painting is shield-shaped on a square wooden frame. The church is shown on the top half, with the old trees framing it. The bottom part shows other local landmarks of historical interest. The sign can be found outside the church.

HEIGHINGTON

Heighington lies four miles south east of Lincoln and the name probably means an estate associated with a man called Hyht. In 1242 it was called Hictinton. The village has a millstream running through it and is incorporated into the design on the village sign, curving under the bridge, through the village and up to the Old Mill, depicted by a mill-wheel.

The attractive wrought-iron sign shows the name done in fancy lettering at the top, making this unusual, forming the top of a shield-shape.
Below the name open country is depicted, with the Church above the bridge.
Although the village has now been excessively developed, after being designated as a Lincoln 'main village', and has adequate shopping and leisure facilities, there remain treasures from the past.

The visitor may wonder why the church stands in the village playground! It was built originally in Norman times, but when James I was on the throne, it had fallen into disuse. Thomas Garrett, who bought local land and was a pioneer in draining it, also founded a village school. For the purpose, he renovated the old church, which is why it has an adjoining schoolroom as well as a unique chapel of ease. When a new school was built in the eighteen hundreds, the church resumed its proper use as a place of worship. The tower is 13th. century.
There is a Victorian Methodist Chapel nearby. Fine stone houses have also stood the test of time.
The shield-shape of the sign is cupped at the base by black scroll embellishments, attractively ending at the top in gold leaves or maybe flames.

HOLBEACH

Holbeach was listed in the Domesday Book and it means 'hollow stream or ridge'. It is now a small market town with one main street with the Church of All Saints in the middle.

Holbeach has had at least five different village signs.

Three of the signs show the Church of All Saints with its steeple, and in all instances show a lot of trees round it. One sign shows a stork and bulrushes; another shows two daffodils in front of a ploughed field, reflecting the bulb growing industry of the area, which has been likened to Holland; another shows

a duck followed by her three chicks and mate, all walking on a road and passing market stalls with canvas roofs, and beneath the name are three red tulips, again reflecting the area's industry. All of these signs have the crown crest of Sezanne, with which Holbeach is twinned..

Another sign is divided into four parts with one showing a church, one showing the crest of Sezanne, another a town crest, whilst fourth shows the Nobel Peace Medal. On the top of this there appears to be a millstone.

A fifth sign is made with leaded glass. It depicts the windmill, a bell tower, the steepled

church, a horse-drawn wagon with children, ducks, watering cans, and two men working on the soil perhaps making a water channel.

12

Besides all of these, the town crest, old and new versions, can be found swinging from the Holbeach beacon.

There is evidence of Roman occupation in the town, and the Charter was given in 1252. The market and Fairs were established by Thomas de Multon, whose family were 12th century Lords of Holbeach. The de Kirtons came next and established a hospital in 1351 opposite the church. The ruins of that were removed by Antiquary William Stukely in the 17th.century. Henry Rands, one of the compilers of the Prayer Book, called himself Henry Holbeach on entering Crowland Abbey. He became Bishop of Lincoln in 1547. Susannah Centlivre, nee Freeman, was one of our earliest women writers. Born in 1667, she wrote her first play aged 23, married Joseph Centlivre , who was a chef to Queen Anne and George I, 6 years later. After that she wrote a play a year up to her death in 1723. Noted for her comedy and humorous plots, one of Garrick's favourite roles was in one of her plays.

Holbeach has one principal street running east to west with the Church of All Saints in the centre and other smaller streets running on the North & South sides.

The church , on the south side of the main street, is of the decorated period 1290 to 1350, probably nearer 1350. There have been at least three major restorations carried out that are known. The restorations by Ewan Christian especially to the chancel were carried out 1859 - 1860. The top of the spire was rebuilt and the chancel re- roofed in 1866 - 1868 and in 1871 - 1873 the chancel was re fitted.

The reredos was by Wilfrid Bond in 1913. The font is octagonal perpendicular style with a panelled stem. Around the bowl are angels with shields and instruments of the passion, unfortunately these have been damaged. The pulpit of 1872 was designed by Ewan Christian, the rood of 1930 by Wilfrid Bond and the organ case in 1950 by Lawrence Bond.

There is a praying effigy of Sir Humphrey Littlebury late 14th Century. The tomb chest has deep niches similar to kneeling niches and is attributed to Bristol craftsmen. There is a similar monument in Bristol Cathedral of Lord Berkeley who died in 1368. There is a 30 inch long part brass to an early 15th Century Knight and one to Joanna Welby, on a tomb chest, She died in 1488. In the chancel on the north side is a wall tablet with books on the top to Philip Ashby who died in 1794, by Henson of Spalding.

HORNCASTLE

The name of the town comes from the fact that it lies where the Rivers Bain and Waring meet, leaving a horn-shaped piece of land. The 'castle' comes from the Roman fort, which was called Banovallum. It also played an important part in the Civil War, when the Cavaliers were attacking Hull in 1643. The Roundheads advanced to help, besieging Bolingbroke Castle on the way. Fairfax had occupied Horncastle for Parliament and 75 Cavalier troops and 5000 foot soldiers came from Lincoln, so Fairfax had to fall back and helped Cromwell, who had 37 Horse Troops with 6000 on foot attending them. The famous battle took place at Winceby, on high ground between Horncastle and Spilsby. The Cavaliers retreated to Newark. Cromwell had nearly died, having his horse shot from under him. Bolingbroke was forced to surrender and the Parliamentarians had won.

The town's August Horse Fair was evocatively described in George Borrow's The Romany Rye.

The medieval church of St. Mary has been restored and partially rebuilt. The tower is 13th and 15th century with a 19th century leaded spire. There is a chest of 1690 and a case containing some old chained books. There are also 13 scythe blades which were either used at the Battle of Winceby or in the Lincolnshire Rising in the defence of the monasteries later.

A brass on the N. aisle shows the 'King's Champion', Sir Lionel Dymoke in 1519, kneeling in his armour, worn when he entered Westminster Hall to challenge in battle anyone who denied the monarch's right to the throne of England.

Horncastle Market Place boasts a monument to Edward Stanhope, MP for Horncastle who served under Disraeli and Lord Salisbury. Dated 1894, it bears plaques containing his portrait and coat of arms.

Sellwood house, in the corner of the market place, was the home of Emily Sellwood, whom Tennyson met when she was 17. Their courtship lasted 20 years, until his poetry brought him in enough to marry on, but she was faithful and waited. She had her reward, as the couple were blessed with children.

The attractive village sign is shield-shaped, with the nameplate curved around the town crest. Below is depicted much of the history, including the Stanhope memorial, old buildings, the horse fair, a Roman soldier, wildlife and agricultural motifs, as well as a scroll stating that this has been a market Town since 1231 and is twinned with Bonnetable, with the crest on the top of the post.

INGOLDMELLS

Listed in the Domesday Book, the village name means 'sand banks of a man called Ingjaldr. It is the most easterly of Lincolnshire's villages.

The village sign is divided into three. Two show the six-mile golden beach that begins at Ingoldmells and ends at Gibraltar Point, where there are 1,200 acres of bird sanctuary.

The third part shows a castle, denoting the Roman settlement here. Remains of the long rampart can be traced along the coast, There are also Iron Age salt-works which have been discovered ten foot below the sea.

About a century ago some ancient potteries were seen at low tide. They were round kilns with two-foot thick walls, about fifteen feet across which were identified as either Roman or pre-historic.

The Church of St. Peter and St. Paul is chiefly medieval,. The three stages of the finely buttressed tower represents the three main building periods: the pillared fine thirteenth century nave, the fourteenth century clerestory and windows in the aisles along with more modern additions. The south wall has gabled buttresses and delicate traceries on the windows, whilst the font is 600 years old. By it, set in the floor, are fragments of medieval gravestones. There is one to William of Skegness in 1508. There is a rare brass portrait in the floor of the south aisle to William Palmer, a cripple who died in 1520. His crutch (ye stylt) is shown at his side.

The sign has been seen attached to a wall and also free-standing on a post.

LONG SUTTON

Long Sutton was mentioned in the Domesday book, but the Romans were here before that and have protected the village from the sea with the ancient embankment. Between fen and marsh, boasts four village signs, all of them showing the lovely church of St. Mary.

Sutton is a very common place-name, meaning 'south of another settlement' and the 'Long' affix refers to the length of the parish rather than the length of the road running through it. It is certainly not flat, with Bull Hill being over twenty feet above seas level and Pop Bottle Bridge, so called because it has a pop bottle top built into it, is only eight foot lower.

The church, built in the twelfth century, has a lead spire, 162 foot high, crowned by a golden ball weather vane on top. Crafted in a herringbone pattern of lead on wood, it is reputed to be the finest example of its kind. The church has an upper room, once used as a school, now housing a library. A vestry table, dated 1702, of inlaid work depicting the Holy Spirit in the form of a dove surrounded by flames of fire, was once the canopy of a pulpit given to Lutton Church by Dr. Busby, the famous Westminster schoolmaster. A brass plaque pays tribute to three members of the Winter family, who successively served as organist and choirmaster for a total of 122 years.

There is an annual themed Flower Festival and beside one of the signs can be found plaques to commemorate winning the *East Midlands in Bloom* competition and getting the prize for the *Best Kept Small Town.*

The signs have obviously been repainted over the years, since some photographs show a white scroll commemorating the Charter given by King John, whilst others are in parchment colour. The oldest one is of the church with a crest containing a wheat sheaf and the name plate below. Later designs show the windmill on one, a water pump on another and Black Bess on the third.

One has a small plaque with the words, "Peel School" flanking a pot of red roses. There are red roses incorporated into stained glass in the Church of St. Mary, to remember the Duke of Lancaster connection. John of Gaunt once owned the

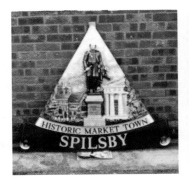

manor. New roads in the town also commemorate the past, for example, Lancaster Drive, near John of Gaunt's House; Turpin Way, York Ride and Sadler's Way.

Famous highwayman, Dick Turpin lived here as John Palmer (Palmer was his mother's maiden name.). In 1737 Turpin linked up with Tom King, another highwayman but during a fight with the police who were trying to arrest them for stealing a horse, Turpin accidentally shot King dead. He managed to get away and went to Louth,

where he lived in High Street and spent his time stealing horses and then selling them on to a local farmer who lived in the mansion was not particular where the horses came from. The authorities came to suspect Turpin's activities and was about to arrest him, when he escaped by riding to York. His famous ride to York on the back of Black Bess was an invention of the novelist, W Harrison Ainsworth.

LOUTH

Louth gets its name from the River Lud, "the noisy stream" and existed at least from Domesday Book times. This old market town's Church of St James has a late Gothic steeple rising to 300 feet high. It is shown on all nine of Louth's town signs, on the approach roads to this historical place. Turner painted it as a backcloth to his picture of the Horse Fair. The tower houses eight bells and it was from this church that came the sermon inciting the Pilgrimage of Grace and 20,000 Lincolnshire men took up arms to defend the monasteries. Henry VIII quickly suppressed this rebellion and its vicar and 60 men from Louth were hanged at Tyburn.

Roman coins and Saxon urns have been found here and it has a long history.

Louth is twinned with the French town of La Ferte Bernard and this is also documented on the signs. Two of them show a horseman with the words, "Sept 21 1551 Edward VI Charter", commemorating the town's Charter and its Royal donor.

Another shows Bishop Alexander with his mitre. It was he who built Newark, Banbury and Sleaford Castles, as well as extending his cathedral at Lincoln. He allowed monks from Fountains Abbey to settle here and in 1139 the bishop built the largest and most magnificent Cisterian Abbey, measuring 256 by 128 feet. The abbey was destroyed soon after the Dissolution, and all that remains of it are parts of a chancel wall, mounds and dykes.

Louth is justly proud of its steepled church, judging from its presence on most of the signs, two of which also record its name, St. James

Another version of the sign carries a white horse and a brown shire horse ploughing, to emphasise the agricultural environments of the town. Louth has had the busiest cattle market in Lincolnshire for centuries.

Inside the church tower is the complete machinery of a four-faced clock with a capability of chiming the hours and partitions of the hours, but you will see no clock face. The machinery was given by one of the important business people of Louth on condition that there were no clock faces to show the time to the workers in the district, who might be tempted to waste time, looking to see if it was time to stop work!

Captain John Smith of Pocahontas fame is also remembered. He went to school here, as did Alfred, Lord Tennyson and his brothers.

Sir John Bolle built Thorpe Hall - he was the hero of the ballad, 'The Spanish Lady of High Degree'. The ghost of a Green Lady is said to still haunt the old hall, but she never saw six-pint-Smith - known as a drunkard and boaster. Almost daily he ordered six and a half pints of beer and on first stroke of 12 downed the first and drank all 12 before the 12th stroke. One day a pedlar came to Louth. He had some goods which Smith wanted but did not have enough money to buy. So Smith challenged the pedlar to a drinking contest. If Smith won, he was to have the goods free. The pedlar agreed and they went to the pub and explained their wager to the landlord, who set two pints before each man and gave the signal to start. Before Smith had drank one pint, the pedlar had downed two. Two more pints were set before each man and again the pedlar downed both before Smith. The contents continued until each man had drank eight pints each. Smith was getting desperate so the pedlar offered him one more chance. He told Smith that if he, Smith, would drink two more pints and then climb the church steeple and hang his hat on the weather vane on top, he could have the goods. Smith readily agreed, drank two more pints, staggered out of the pub, across to the church and slowly began to climb the steeple. After a long hard climb he reached the top, put his hat on the weather

vane and started the long descent. When he got to the ground he almost crawled back into the pub to find the pedlar had gone, taking with him Smith's coat and leaving Smith to pay for the twenty pints of beer they had drank. Thereafter Smith was known as Ten Pint Smith.

19

MOULTON

Moulton, means 'farmstead of a man called Mula' or 'place where mules are kept'.

The village is crowned by it's splendid church, All Saints, eight hundred years old, which is known as the 'Queen of the Fens'. It houses three fonts: an ancient one of stone, an 'Adam and Eve' one and a Victorian one, which you can't miss. There is a note-worthy rood screen and a crocketed spire, one of the many fine examples to be seen in Lincolnshire. Although the church dates from 1180, the tower and beautiful spire were 1300s additions.

Moulton Castle fell into ruins in the 15th. century, but there is still a three-foot high Elloe Stone, marking the place where the Saxon Court of Assembly met. The eight-storey mill near the Church, which is thought to be the tallest in the country and is a landmark for many miles around, is shown on the Moulton sign.

Moulton Grammar School was founded in 1550, and amalgamated with Spalding Grammar School in 1939. Opposite the church, all that now remains of it is Harrox House.

The village school is now a thriving Community Centre, used by the many clubs and societies, youth groups etc. The old Station buildings were turned into a guest-house, popular with the tulip fields tourists.

The Moulton sign was designed by 13-year-old Rebecca Rayner, who won a competition a s at Moulton Seas End, using the same manufacturers. All three Moulton signs well document the history, agricultural and horticultural aspects of Moulton.

MOULTON SEAS END

Moulton Seas End sign was designed by 13-year old Nathan Harries. Nathan won the competition for young people to submit ideas for their village sign organised by Moulton Parish Council. The sign stands in Earlsfield, Moulton Seas End, and was made locally by Roger and Jack Barnes of Moulton Chapel and Harry Dean & Sons in Moulton Seas End.

NETTLEHAM

Nettleham is a large village with a population of a small town. It lies 4 miles N.E. of Lincoln. The name means, predictably, 'homestead or enclosure where nettles

grow'.

Nettleham has some beautiful scenery, with the Beck running through the heart of the village , attracting much wildlife, such as ducks and moorhens. There are footpaths and a Village Trail.

There was an Inclosure Award for Nettleham in 1778

The village has a rich history, going back more than 2000 years, The manor of Nettleham became the property of William the Conqueror after the Norman Conquest and, on his death, it passed to Queen Maud by inheritance. In 1100AD it was handed over by charter to the Bishops of Lincoln whereupon it became a country seat with the manor house being considerably enlarged to accommodate visitors, including the retinues of kings, up to the late 16th century. After the Lincolnshire Rebellion against the Church Reforms of Henry Vlll in 1536, the palace fell into disrepair.

An important archaeological hoard was discovered in Nettleham, in 1860, which is now in the British Museum. There were 4 palstaves, a leaf-shaped spearhead, a basal-looped spearhead, a tubular ferrule from a spear shaft and two socketed axe-heads. All have been certified as Early to Middle Bronze Age. All of this history is depicted on one side of the attractive village sign, whilst the other shows the more pastoral side of the village.

John Wesley, the founder of Methodism, was born in Lincolnshire in 1703, but it was not until 1776 that the new Group reached Nettleham. Lincoln was the furthest reaches of the village and even in the 19th century, it was only when gypsies, tinkers, pedlars and such tradespeople passed through that news came of wider happenings.

The skills of the blacksmith, baker, miller, brewer and joiner were still in demand. Socially, the men fared better that the women, for ale-houses were by now well established. Women sought their entertainment with feasts and the parish events.

The parish church of All Saints stands in the middle of the village in a setting of ancient trees. Of Saxon origin, it has undergone several changes over the centuries, but still contains Medieval wall paintings, decorated Victorian ceiling, several colourful stained glass windows and a magnificent modern east window (replacing an earlier one damaged by fire in 1969). All Saints has a lively membership and activities.

In 1905, following the Typhoid epidemic in Lincoln, it was proposed that the citizens of Lincoln be allowed to "procure water from the Parish Pump for their private use".
Lincoln Police Headquarters are on the outside of the village.

NORTH COCKERINGTON

The village is north-east of Louth and is part of the area known as Middle Marsh. The name means 'farmstead by a stream called Cocker' with the point of the compass direction before it, since there is also a South Cockerington.

This village sign matches and complements the Alvingham sign, fashioned by the same manufacturer. It is made of metal and depicts its name in gold lettering above silhouettes of an owl riding on a tractor, to denote the country and agricultural aspects of the village, the ancient Priory and the two churches .

These are the village Church of St. Mary and St. Adelwold's of nearby Alvington, since both churches share the same churchyard. Obviously this was not overfilled in the Black Death, since the village also has a plaque pit.

In the 12th. century Gilbert of Sempringham, son of a Norman baron, founded a priory here in 1130, next to the site of the earlier Saxon church. (Compare with Alvingham sign text) and at an early date the Church of St. Mary was given to North Cockerington, whose own church had fallen into ruin. St. Mary's, now cared for by the Redundant Churches Trust, has an 18th century tower and chancel arch. There is the top of a Norman window in the North wall of the chancel. The font is set on the base of a Norman pillar and is early 14th. century.

22

OLD BOLINGBROKE

The name means 'brook at Bola's or Bula's place'.

This quiet village was once a thriving market town, with a Norman castle, now in ruins, with only the foundations left to tell its rich history. Around 1220 it passed into the House of Lancaster, via various marriages and so to John of Gaunt, famous fourth son of Edward 111 and Queen Phillippa. After the death of his brother, The Black Prince, he became Regent of England on behalf of the ill-fated Richard II, his young nephew. The throne later passed to John's son, Henry of Bolingbroke, who was born in the castle and later became Henry IV in 1399, well documented by William Shakespeare. Eventually the Castle was uninhabited, becoming a centre of administration for the Duchy of Lancaster and falling into decay.

Geoffrey Chaucer was a frequent visitor to John and Blanche, writing a commemorative poem to Blanche after her death, entitled' The Book of the Duchess' .

The Civil War saw its untimely end, when attacked by Cromwell. Bolingbroke, a Royalist stronghold held out against a siege by Parliamentary troops from Horncastle until the Royalists were defeated in 1643 at the nearby Battle of Winceby. Parliamentary authorities ordered the destruction of the castle and much of the stone was clandestinely removed into the village, where homes were built with it.

The Church of St. Peter and St. Paul was situated too close to the castle to escape damage. It was originally three times as big as now, but after that attack only the south aisle remained, This was patched up, along with what remained of the tower, to become the present church, but in 1363 when it was built, it must have been an impressive sight. There are two old worn heads by the old doorway of the church, believed to be the parents of John of Gaunt, Edward III and Queen Philippa.

In a triangular plot outside the church you will find the double-sided village sign, with the arms of the Duchy of Lancaster. There is an association with France and so the roses planted around the sign, roses of Provins, were a gift from the people of France.

The sign shows on one side Henry of Bolingbroke and on the other the Duke of Lancaster, with the family Coat of Arms.

POTTERHANWORTH

Potterhanworth, on the northern side of the county, means 'pot-making here in the enclosure of a man called Hana'. There was a Roman encampment here, with a pottery and their wares have been unearthed ever since. The 14th century church of St. Andrew was rebuilt in 1854 and designed by Hussey, to replace the earlier one of 1749. One of the bells was recast for Queen Victoria's Diamond Jubilee and was engraved with words of Alfred, Lord Tennyson:

The old order changeth, yielding place to new;
And God fulfills Himself in many ways
Lest one good custom should corrupt the world.

There is a window in the church depicting Moses the Law-maker, to commemorate the life of Lord Chancellor Campbell, a great lawyer, who wrote long books on the works of past Chief Justices and Chancellors.

The double-sided village sign depicts some of this history, including the bell, the book and coat of arms, pilgrims to the church, as well as a windmill, horse drawn plough and other pastoral scenes. All set into a solid wooden frame, it is an attractive sign for a lovely village

SAXILBY

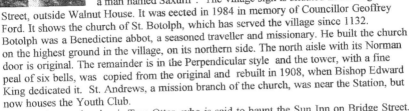

Saxilby-with-Ingleby lies six miles north-west of Lincoln on the A57, twelve miles from Gainsborough. Today it is a thriving village, with nine times the population of former days. The name comes from the Viking warrior Saxult, who invaded the village and means a 'farmstead or village of a man named Saxulfr'. The village sign is situated in the High Street, outside Walnut House. It was eected in 1984 in memory of Councillor Geoffrey Ford. It shows the church of St. Botolph, which has served the village since 1132. Botolph was a Benedictine abbot, a seasoned traveller and missionary. He built the church on the highest ground in the village, on its northern side. The north aisle with its Norman door is original. The remainder is in the Perpendicular style and the tower, with a fine peal of six bells, was copied from the original and rebuilt in 1908, when Bishop Edward King dedicated it. St. Andrews, a mission branch of the church, was near the Station, but now houses the Youth Club.

The poacher on the sign is Tom Otter, who is said to haunt the Sun Inn on Bridge Street. He married his wife, Mary in 1806 but love was short-lived, since he murdered her on the same day! Each anniversary, ghostly movements and noises are heard, they say.

You can find Tom Otter's Lane about a mile from the village (towards Drinsey Nook). His body hung here from a gibbet after his trial and execution. The gibbet collapsed forty odd years later, but the gibbet irons can still be seen at Doddington Hall.

The sign also depicts a Lincoln Red, the locally-bred cow, in spite of the fact that Lincoln is more associated with green! The sailing barge also depicted shows how important the river was to the village. You can still arrive by boat, as the Romans did. They dug the Foss Dyke to link up with the River Trent at Torksey Lock, thus accessing trade in the Midlands and the Humber Estuary. This extended the use of the River Witham and Brayford Pool. The river still plays a significant part, with picnic areas and walks, angling, and easy access across a former railway footbridge to moorings and other activities. The Danes invaded from the River, lead by Saxult, so a diversity of craft and people have arrived at Saxilby by water.

The Jarrow marchers stayed a night in Saxilby, camping in a large building named the 'White City', a local hall used for community events, standing where the Ship Inn car park now is. The villagers rallied round the marchers, providing meals and blankets, whilst the two village cobblers repaired their shoes, sending them on their way with fresh provisions and cheery good wishes.

The existing village hall was once one of four chapels and was extended and refurbished in 1975. The old village school is now commercial premises. The new Methodist Church was built in 1940, replacing an earlier chapel.

Rose Bearings, of world-wide renown has brought industry and expansion to the village. Its products are used in Concorde, the car racing industry, space travel, etc. It expanded and moved to Lincoln, just ten minutes away by train. The Victorian station is no longer used, but new properties arose from the site of the old engine shed. . There is a black and white half-timbered 16th. century cottage in the High Street, reputably a cruck-frame dwelling.

SLEAFORD

Sleaford's sign boasts that it has been a market town since 1120AD. Indeed, it existed before then and was listed in the Domesday Book.. Sleaford got its name from having a 'ford over a muddy stream', now known as the River Slea. The sign shows shire horses pulling a laden wagon and being guided by a man. Behind this is a delicately steepled church, and town buildings are depicted at rear and sides of the church. One building looks like an ancient inn complete with a sign. An inn in Southgate has a sign showing dog-baiting by a tethered bull, a 'sport' of former days. The other building on the left is the timber-built Carre Hospital, a group of 17th century almshouses founded by Sir Robert Carre, whose family's charitable works are remembered at the Sleaford Grammar School. There are similar almshouses in Northgate, near the Grammar School.

The magnificent Church of St Denis looks more like a cathedral and has one of England's earliest stone spires. Its windows are renowned for some of the finest flowing tracery that can be found in any English parish church. However arguably the church's greatest treasure is its screen, along with an embroidered altar carpet, woven in silk and wool at the Sheldon factory in Barchester, Warwickshire. Thought to have been made around 1620, it is mentioned in the churchwardens records for 1628. It is now framed and hangs in the North aisle. There are also eight bells, made in Norfolk by Thomas Osborne and, more unusually, a medieval 'butter bell', which was used for the Market and is the only one still in existence.

The town is the meeting point for numerous roads and railway lines. It was probably always a busy place, with a Roman station here, since a vast Roman/Anglo cemetery was discovered when the railway line was extended. Ornaments, weapons and pieces of pottery were found, many now in the British Museum.

After Domesday, the Bishops of Lincoln played a more prominent part in the history of the town. William the Conqueror gave the manor to Remigius, the first Bishop. Around 1130 AD Bishop Alexander built the Castle and King Stephen seized it, but it was later returned to the See. King John spent a night there on his way to Newark Castle, where he died. Bishop Fleming, the Founder of Lincoln College, Oxford, died here in 1431. Henry Holbeach of Lincoln, one of the compilers of the Prayer Book, finally gave up the Castle and Sleaford manor. It was appropriated by Protector Somerset for the Crown. Queen Mary later gave the castle and manor to Admiral Lord Clinton. The Carre family were the next owners, before it was pulled down in the late Elizabethan period.

Old Place was the home of Lord Hussey, a distinguished Lord Chief Justice of England through the reigns of three Kings, well rewarded by Henry VIII. He was executed by Cromwell. The old timbered Rectory has a carved date of 1568.

There has been a long and rich history to portray on the sign.

SKEGNESS

Skegness, at the end of the A52 about 12 miles N.E. of Boston, is well known as a seaside resort, since the 9th Earl of Scarborough, appreciating its six miles of beach and bracing sea air, began planning it as a holiday resort in 1877. In the 12th. century, the town was a tiny fishing village known as Sceggenesse, meaning 'Beard-shaped promontory', 'promontory of a man called Skeggi' and 'Skeggie' it is affectionately called by the thousands of visitors who flock here each year.

Lord Tennyson and his brothers, who went to Louth Grammar School, loved to fish here. The town sign is really only a welcome sign, not portraying the history of Roman ramparts, poets musings and Earl's planning, pier construction or railway expansion and the like, but a picture post-card-type 'Welcome to Skegness', written over an inviting tourist picture of golden sands, cloudless sky and blue sea. Beneath is another board promoting Natureland Seal Sanctuary, with the information that it is open every day. Yet this encompasses the plans the Earl saw coming to fruition, as he organised the making of thirty-four acres of seafront gardens, with thousands of roses and other summer blooms. The ambitious pier construction was completed in 1881, said to be 1843 foot long. (Now just another 38 feet and we would have had the date imprinted on our minds too!) Sadly the pier was swept away, along with much else along the East coast, in the 1987 notorious gales, but the gardens were restored to their former glory in time for the next summer season.

The first holiday camp was established here and the popularity of Butlins soon spread. The old Church of St. Clement stands half a mile inland, in a beautifully wooded churchyard. It is a quaint little building from the 1400s, with an earlier arch in the square sturdy tower. The carved font is over 500 years old, with tracery and shields still visible. It is a typical little village church, without the ornamentation and long crocheted spires of many other Lincolnshire towns, but it has seen millions of worshippers over the years.

The first railway line was built in 1873, enabling more ordinary families to come to the seaside. With the Industrial Revolution and more work, including an annual holiday, the Earl of Scarborough's foresight brought the healthy delights of the seaside to people who had never before seen the sea.

The aerodrome is near the bank the Romans built to protect the land from the sea, part of the thirty-mile rampart, still visible in parts along the coast, from Boston to Sutton-on-Sea.

SKELLINGTHORPE

Skellingthorpe, west of Lincoln, shows the old spelling of Scheldinchape on the reverse side of its village sign, given to the parish by the W.I. to commemorate their Diamond Jubilee in 1982. The name means 'enclosure in marsh of a farmstead belonging to a man called Sceld' or a 'shield-shaped enclosure. Formerly a small agricultural village, it did export fowl to London, where Skellingthorpe Duck' was apparently a delicacy. Ducks and rabbits probably formed the staple diet of the residents, since the soil was poor.

The more modern history of the village, including a World War II aeroplane, is recorded on the side of the sign with the modern nameplate. Henry Stone's coat of Arms, carved in stone on the Stone Arms public house, is featured on the historical side . The inn was flooded to six foot high when the Spalford Bank burst in the 1700s. Women travelled to Lincoln Market by boat for several weeks until the water subsided.

Henry Stone was Lord of the Manor, but having no heir, left the land to Christ's Hospital, London in 1693. Day schools came into being in the 1850s and all landowners paid into the Spital Charity, which helped poorer scholars. Today the Trust supplies a Bible to every child leaving the village school, shown on the sign, along with Skellingthorpe Hall and the Church of St. Lawrence, as well as lots of agricultural and wildlife.

There was a railway service from 1896 to 1980, when the line closed. Coal used to come from the Midlands and fish from Grimsby, as well as the passenger service, also depicted on the sign. A Community Centre and Youth Hall now stands on the station site, which belongs to the Parish Council. The old Lamplighter's hut is used as a store, but they say it still reeks of paraffin!

This was one of Lincolnshire's largest parishes, with the Old Wood reputed to be part of Sherwood Forest. The western border meets the Nottingham border.

Lincoln City took over the old aerodrome land after the war and there is a large Birchwood Estate built there.

SPALDING

Spalding has one main double-sided sign, carved by famous early sign-maker, the late Harry Carter, with four others, all alike, at the gateway to the town on the approach roads.

Spalding has existed at least from Domesday Book times and gets its name from an old word meaning ditch or trench. The town has now the River Welland flowing through it and seven bridges to cross it, which gives it a Dutch appearance.

One side of the main sign shows a man holding a book, and the other shows three men in animated discussion. These depict Maurice Johnson who founded the Gentlemen's Society of Spalding in 1710, a social club to encourage study of scientific and literary subjects and was the forerunner of the Society of Antiquaries. The Spalding Gentlemen's Society with its library and museum of antiquities is now on Broad Street. The Society also owns the Bird Museum in Red Lion Street, from which hundreds of specimens were moved to Ayscoughfee Hall, dating from the 15th century. Incorporated in the sign's spandrels holding the name place are yellow, white and red tulips. The area surrounding Spalding supports more than half of England's bulb growing, as well as growing acres of potatoes, sugar beet and other root vegetables and has been dubbed the most fertile area in the country. Above the name place is a crest with the motto, "vicinas urbes alit".

The other of Spalding's signs, the 'gateway' version, has a woman in a blue dress tending tulips. This scene is surmounted by the same crest and motto as that on the sign in the town centre. Underneath is a twinning notice - surprisingly, not with a town in Holland, but with a German town, Speyer.

Spalding is the last town on the Welland, before it enters the Wash and the most important of Fenland towns. It was named in the Crowland Abbey foundation charter and is said to have had a wooden chapel in the 9th. century. Spalding Priory was established in the mid-11th. century by Thorold of Buckenhale, brother of Lady Godiva. Originally a cell of Crowland, it was eventually expanded and transferred to the Abbey of Angers, starting a dissension between Crowland and Spalding that was to last well into the 14th. century. It resumed its independence however, and entertained Kings Edward I and II, John of Gaunt and his friend Geoffrey Chaucer.

Spalding Castle stood to the north of the town, but the crowning glory of the town is the beautiful church of St. Mary and St. Nicholas, of 1284, complete with impressive tower and spire.

SPILSBY

Called Spilisbi in 1086, the name means 'village or farmstead of a man called Spilir. Situated at the southern end of the Lincolnshire Wolds, there has been a Market here since the 14th. century. There is a market cross, with the base and steps being over 600 years old. In the Market Place there is a bronze statue of famous explorer Sir John Franklin. He holds a telescope in one hand and the other rests on an anchor. He was a cousin of Matthew Flinders, of Donnington and they both joined the Navy when they were only 14. He was therefore involved in the survey of Australia, sailing with Captain Bligh of the Bounty. He was engaged in the Battle of Trafalgar at 19 and undertook his Arctic exploration when 32 years old, discovering the N.W. Passage. . He was Governor of New Zealand after his three and five year voyages, but the Arctic drew him back and he was lost there in 1847. Thirty-five ships searched for him and his party. He was never found, but two of his men were, in 1925. There is another monument to him in Westminster Abbey. His nephew, Tennyson, wrote the inscription, 'Not here…etc.'

The Spilsby statue is the main feature of Spilsby's traditional sign, an attractive triangular-shaped one, announcing it to be a Historic Market Town, as well as portraying some of that history, in buildings and landscape. There is also a Spilsby Welcome, entry sign, telling us that the town is Franklin's birthplace and that it is twinned with Fresnay-sur-Sarthe and showing the English and French flags.

The town's Charter was obtained by William de Willoughby (near Alford). He married Alice, heiress of Baron Bek of Eresby, founding the great family of William de Eresby. Eresby Hall, a mile south of the town, was burned down in 1769, but a farmhouse was built from the ruins.

The Church of St. James has a 15th century tower, exterior walls encased in Ancaster stone in 1879 and a new south aisle built. There are many fine alabaster figures from 1372.

Kathleen, Baroness Willoughby, married Richard Bertie and Grimstone Castle became the family seat. Since they were zealous for the Reformation, Latimer was entertained there.

SUTTON BRIDGE

This village sign, which commemorates the Silver Jubilee of Queen Elizabeth II, is at the approach of the attractive metal bridge. Indeed a model of the bridge forms part of the sign and rests on the place name. The main part of the sign has four elements in relief. These are a lighthouse, wheat-sheaf, steam train, and fish. Finally, the sign is surmounted by the cross keys of St Peter.

Sutton Bridge is the home of the 'Yellowbellies' as Lincolnshire fenmen used to be called due to the reputation to turn yellow with the distemper. The lighthouse is one of the two standing over the Nene, which were not used for guiding ships, but Peter Scott lived in one of them, East Bank Lighthouse, and thus gained much of his knowledge of birds. The fish depicts the trawling industry on the Nene. The steam train recalls the fact that Robert Stephenson designed the original iron swing-bridge spanning the River Nene, but this was replaced by the present bridge built in 1894.

The village sign is on a small green on the western approach to the bridge.

The village gets its name from Long Sutton. Sutton Bridge was once an important town and was the point of embarkation across the Cross Keys Wash where King John lost his treasure and baggage in 1216. Local gardeners are still hoping to dig some of it up! King John's Farm is where he is supposed to have rested for the night. After getting nearly drowned, this probably hastened his death a few weeks later.

The Crosskeys Swing Bridge, spanning the River Nene, is the focal point of the village and a listed building. R.S & John Rennie built the bridge. The present Bridge was built at the end of the 19th century at a cost of £80,000, unusual in that it operates hydraulically.

A famous Lincolnshire Poacher, Mackenzie Thorpe, known as 'Kenzie the Wild Gooseman', worked for Sir Peter Scott and picked up tips from him on painting. Soon he was producing his own drawings and paintings of local wildlife. His nocturnal habits once landed him in jail and he often clashed with the Royal Gamekeeper at Sandringham. This lead to Prince Charles taking an interest in this character and visiting him in his council house. This led to the street being renamed 'Royal Close'

There have been associations with the RAF here since 1926, when a summer camp for airmen was started, leading to a training unit. The flat land was ideal for coaching pilots and many involved in the Battle of Britain were trained here. Some who died were buried with local men in St. Matthews Church, where the altar in the North aisle is dedicated to them. Their names are carved on an oak plaque.

Disastrous docks were constructed in 1888, but only survived for a month, due to shifting sand under their foundations. They were eventually rebuilt in 1988 and a new port constructed, leading to expansion of the village.

WHAPLODE

Whaplode is a long, scattered village in South-East Lincolnshire. The name means 'channel or watercourse where eel-pouts are found'.

There has been a traditional sign for several years, showing the fine Church of St. Mary, with the name-plate below. (There have been recent additions, two metal signs, one sculpted in the form of a tulip to depict the prolific bulb-growing industry and the other a star. However these are not in Fred Ham's collection, since they are too recent, but will be included in our third book of Lincolnshire signs.)

The church is Norman, 13th-14th century, with a hundred foot long nave, graced by seven elegant arches on each side. There is a beautiful West front doorway and a monument to Sir Anthony Irby of Irby Hall, which is now a farmhouse. He has come down through English literature, since Phineas Fletcher wrote a hundred-stanza elegy to him. The font is modern, but in the Norman style. Whaplode church is another example of the marvellous and impressive places of worship to be found all over this lovely county.

CONTENTS

Page

Introduction

A.L. PUBLICATIONS
52, London Rd., KESSINGLAND, Lowestoft, Suffolk. NR3 7PW
NOW IN PRINT

SUFFOLK SIGNS Books 1, 2, 3 & 4.
By Shirley Addy and Maureen Long
Book 1 – published June 1996   ISBN 0 9527293 0 X
Book 2 – published September 1996   ISBN 0 9527293 1 8
Book 3 – published October 1998   ISBN 0 9527293 3 4
Book 4 – published September 2001   ISBN 0 9527293 7 7
NORFOLK SIGNS Book 4 Philippa Millar   ISBN 0 9527293 8 5
CAMBRIDGESHIRE SIGNS Books 2 & 3 Ian MacEachern
ISBNs 0 9527293 9 3 and 0 9542950 0 5
Each book is in an easy to carry format using A5 glossy paper with many full colo
and black and white photographs. 52pp with colour card cover.
Price £3.99 each.
RIDER HAGGARD AND EGYPT by Shirley M. Addy
ISBN 0 9527293 2 6
Foreword by Dr. A Rosalie David, Keeper of Egyptology, Manchester Museum.
Introduction by Commander Mark Cheyne, DSC, RN. DL Grandson of Sir Henry
Rider Haggard. 186pp. A4 format. Price: £25.
SOME MORE OF MY POEMS by Mary Devereux
ISBN 09527293 4 2   75pp of true –to-life humorous and delightful poems,
in local dialect.   A5 glossy Cover. Price: £3.50.

Two Books by Kessingland Author John Westley (who wrote 'And the Road
Below' an account of his walk round Britain in aid of Multiple Sclerosis, publish
Meridian books –available through A.L. Publications. £8.99)

BURKE'S LORE- Pithy Proverbs of the Kessingland Sage
Illustrated by Suffolk artist Evelyn Mathias
ISBN 0 9527293 5 0   Price :£2.50.

ECLIPSED   ISBN 0 9527293 6 9   Account of John's 400+
mile walk to see the 1999 solar eclipse. With photographs and
illustrations. Price: £3.99.